EXPERIMENT WITH PLANTS

Written by Monica Byles

Science Consultant: Linda Gamlin

Education Consultants: Uschi Spearman and Ruth Bessant

Lerner Publications Company
Minneapolis, Minnesota

All words marked in **bold** can be found in the glossary that begins on page 30.

This edition published in 1994 by:
Lerner Publications Company
241 First Avenue North
Minneapolis, Minnesota 55401

First published in Great Britain in 1992 by:
Two-Can Publishing, 346 Old Street, London EC1V 9NQ

Library of Congress Cataloging-in-Publication Data

Byles, Monica.
    Experiment with plants / written by Monica Byles ; [illustrations by Nancy
Anderson].
       p.   cm.
    Originally published: London : Two-Can Pub., 1992.
    Includes index.
    Summary: Presents basic information on plants and simple experiments that
demonstrate some of their characteristics.
    ISBN 0-8225-2456-2
    1. Botany—Experiments—Juvenile literature. 2. Gardening—Experiments—
Juvenile literature. [1. Plants—Experiments. 2. Experiments.] I. Anderson, Nancy,
ill. II. Title.
QK52.6.B94   1994
581'.078—dc20   92-43117
                                                                              CIP
                                                                              AC

Printed in Hong Kong
Bound in the United States of America

1 2 3 4 5 6 99 98 97 96 95 94

ISBN: 0-8225-2456-2

Photographs are reproduced by permission of Paul Bricknell and Toby Maudsley,
except for the following: cover, Planet Earth/John Lythgoe; p. 4 (bottom), Bruce
Coleman/Jeff Foott; p. 4 (top), Bruce Coleman/Alain Compost; p. 5 (top right), p. 9
(top right), p. 21 (top left), Biofotos/Heather Angel; p. 5 (left), ZEFA/Luis Villota;
p. 6, Bruce Coleman/Dr. Eckart Pott; p. 7, ZEFA/Kohlhas; p. 9 (bottom left), Bruce
Coleman/Eric Crichton; p. 11 (center right), Bruce Coleman/Frithfoto; p. 11 (bottom
center), Bruce Coleman/Jane Burton; p. 12 (left), p. 23 (bottom right), Science Photo
Library/Vaughan Fleming; p. 12 (right), ZEFA/Photo Researchers; p. 12 (bottom left),
Science Photo Library/Dr. Jeremy Burgess; p. 14 (left), Bruce Coleman/Kim Taylor;
p. 15 (left) ZEFA/Starfoto; p. 15 (right), ZEFA/Weir; p. 19 (top), ZEFA/Roy Hamas;
p. 19 (bottom), Science Photo Library/John Heseltine; p. 20, ZEFA/H. Mante; p. 21,
Oxford Scientific Films/Roland Mayr; p. 22 (left), Science Photo Library/Peter Ryan;
p. 25 (top left), Hutchison/Maurice Harvey; p. 25 (center right), Hutchison/Tim
Motion; p. 26 (top left), Hutchison/Michael Macintyre; p. 28, Michael & Patricia Fogden.

Illustrations by Nancy Anderson.

CONTENTS

PLANTS EVERYWHERE

Plants are everywhere—indoors and outdoors, in our gardens and in the wild. Plants grow in the most unlikely places—in cracks in the sidewalk and on old buildings, in dry deserts and under water. Scientists believe that more than 350,000 **species**, or kinds, of plants exist.

▶ Rain forests receive a lot of water and have more different plant species than any

other **habitat**, or home for a group of living things. The world's largest flower is produced by the giant rafflesia plant. The rafflesia grows mainly in the rain forest. This flower can grow to be almost three feet (90 centimeters) across.

◀ The plants we call trees are the largest living things on Earth. Trees grow slowly and can live a very long time. The bristlecone pine trees that grow in the southwestern United States are among the oldest living things in the world. Some of these trees have been alive for 5,000 years!

Many plants grow in rivers, shallow ponds, or oceans. A few water plants are so small that they can only be seen with a microscope. Some types of water plants have pods of air in their leaves or stems. The pods of air act like life preservers and lift the leaves or stems up to the light above the water. All plants need light to survive.

How many different kinds of flowers can you see on this flower seller's boat? About half of all the world's plant species are flowering plants. They come in all different shapes, colors, and sizes—from a tiny, fragile orchid to a huge oak tree.

LIQUID OF LIFE

If you forget to water a plant for a while, it will quickly droop and wilt. A plant cannot live without water. Some plants live in or under water. Other plants, such as cactuses, can grow in parched deserts where very little rain falls. Many desert plants store water in their fleshy stems or leaves.

▶ You can grow plants underwater in a pond you make yourself. Dig a hole and line it with a plastic garbage bag. Add rocks or shape the sides of the hole so that the middle is deeper than the edges. Fill the pond with water and wait a few days. Gather different water plants from a nearby pond or lake, and put them in your pond. Wait a week and see what other plants start growing.

▲ The huge welwitschia plant lives only in the Namib Desert in southwest Africa. When fog drifts across the desert from the Atlantic coast, the welwitschia's leaves **absorb** the tiny water droplets from the fog.

Water lilies can grow in deep water because they have very long stems. Round, flat leaves float on the water's surface and gather sunlight. Strong roots anchor the water lilies to the bottom of the pond.

Cactuses grow best in dry soil, so water them only occasionally. Other plants prefer damp soil, but don't overwater them. Too much water can kill potted plants.

LIGHT FANTASTIC

Plants need energy to grow. They get energy from sunlight. Some plants grow in hot countries where they are exposed to harsh sunlight all day long. Other plants thrive in shady places like forests. But all plants must have some light to survive. What would happen if you left a plant inside a dark closet for a long time?

▼ Make an envelope of construction paper and slide it over one or two leaves of a potted plant. Leave the plant near a window for a week. Take off the paper. What do you see?

Most plants have green leaves. Look more closely, and you will see that some leaves have other colors, too. Leaves with different-colored markings are known as **variegated** leaves. The leaves of **deciduous** trees change color in the fall and drop to the ground. **Evergreen** trees have green leaves all year round.

The plants growing in these window boxes make a colorful display. They get plenty of sunlight to help them grow well.

Have you seen plants reach for the light? Try this experiment with a pot of **seedlings**, or young plant shoots. Stand an open greeting card behind a pot of seedlings on a windowsill. What happens to the seedlings after several hours? What happens if you turn the pot around?

BREATHING OUT

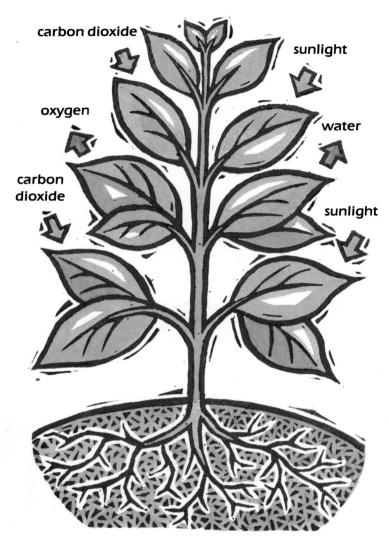

carbon dioxide

sunlight

oxygen

water

carbon dioxide

sunlight

To see photosynthesis at work, try this experiment. Fill a bowl with water and add some weeds from a pond or lake. Then place a jar upside down in the bowl. Tilt the jar to let the air out of it. Push the weeds halfway into the jar, then rest the jar on top of the stems. Leave the bowl in bright sunlight for several hours, then look again. Bubbles of oxygen rise to the water surface. Like all plants, the weeds give off oxygen.

Plants are green because they contain a green-colored substance called **chlorophyll**. Chlorophyll uses energy from sunlight to combine carbon dioxide from the air with water to make food for the plant. This complex process, called **photosynthesis**, usually takes place in a plant's leaves. Excess water and oxygen, by-products of photosynthesis, are released into the air. All living things, including people, need oxygen to survive.

◀ Put a clear plastic bag over a potted plant and seal it around the stem with string. Leave the plant in sunlight for a day. When you remove the bag, you will see water droplets on the leaves. Tiny holes in the leaves absorb carbon dioxide, but water is also lost through these holes. Many leaves have a waxy coating to help keep water in.

▶ Mangrove trees grow in swampy coastal areas. The tree's long, spreading roots anchor it in the water.

◀ Along with air, water, and light, plants need **minerals** to grow. Some plants do not find the minerals they need in the soil. Instead, these plants eat insects and take in the minerals from their bodies! Here, a fly lands on a Venus flytrap. As the fly brushes sensitive hairs on the plant's leaves, the plant's "jaws" snap shut.

FLOWER POWER

Plants and animals help each other survive. Animals help plants **reproduce**, or make new plants. Plants provide animals with food.

▲ Watch a busy bee travel from flower to flower. Pollen from one flower sticks to the bee and is carried to another flower.

The special colors, shapes, and smells of flowers send signals to insects, birds, or bats — telling them where to pick up or deposit pollen.

▲ When a hummingbird visits a flower, it is looking for the sweet **nectar** inside. **Pollen** from the flower sticks to the bird's beak and brushes off on other flowers the bird visits. Pollen is made up of tiny grains that help plants reproduce.

Pollen is produced in the male parts of a flower, or **stamens**. Petals and sepals protect and support the flower's reproductive parts. When pollen is carried to a flower with female reproductive parts, pollen grains join with female cells inside the flower, and seeds begin to form. The seeds can then grow into new plants.

petal

stamen

sepal

The fragrances of flowers appeal to people as well as to birds and insects. Perfume is made from flowers such as jasmine and roses. Experiment with different scents to perfume your room. Gather flowers from garden plants like rosemary, lavender, and roses. Dry the petals between paper towels, then arrange them in a bowl.

SEEDS AND SPORES

When a plant makes seeds, it must scatter them so that new young plants will grow. Some seeds travel by sailing on the wind. Others are spread by animals.

▲ Plants such as mosses and ferns grow from **spores** instead of seeds. Brown lumps on the underside of fern leaves produce millions of tiny spores. The wind may carry the dustlike spores a long way from the parent plant before they take root.

◄ All seeds are surrounded by a protective **seed coat**. In some plants, the seed coat is very hard. As seeds develop, they are held and protected inside the **fruit** of the plant. Many fruits, such as apples and cherries, are fleshy and juicy when they ripen.

If a fruit is eaten by an animal, the seed then passes through the animal's body and falls to the ground in its droppings. If the seed has good soil and enough water and sunlight, it will **germinate**, or split open and start to grow. Many seeds have a built-in food supply, which the seedling uses until it grows big enough to make its own food.

Seeds like chestnuts have a tough skin that keeps them from rotting. Squirrels bury nuts for their winter food supply. Some of these nuts are lost or forgotten. In the spring, they may sprout where they were buried and take root.

▲ Watch a pinecone to predict the weather. A closed pinecone is a sign that rain may be coming. If the pinecone is open, the weather will be warm and dry. Pinecones open to release their seeds in sunny weather.

▼ Remove the stalk from a mushroom. Leave the top on a piece of white paper overnight. Lift it to see the pattern left by spores produced by the mushroom.

Never eat mushrooms you find outdoors. They may be poisonous.

15

SPROUTING SEEDS

Some seeds grow inside pods. When the pods are ripe, they burst open, shooting the seeds out in many directions. Depending on where a seed lands, months or even years may pass before conditions are right for the seed to germinate. Seeds need water and warmth to germinate and grow into adult plants.

▼ It's easy to make seeds sprout at home. Stand a large potato in a container. Make a hole in the top of the potato, and sprinkle mustard seeds or mung beans in it. You can buy most seeds and beans at the grocery store. Attach vegetable slices with toothpicks to make a face. The water in the potato will make the seeds sprout. After a few days, you should have a hairy potato head.

▼ Loosely roll a paper towel and put it in a jar. Wet the paper towel and keep it damp. Put a fresh kidney bean between the glass and the paper, about halfway up the jar. In a few days, the seed coat should begin to split, and you'll see a shoot and small roots poking out. Each day, make a mark on the side of the jar to keep track of how much the shoot and root have grown.

▲ Soak a cupful of mung beans in water overnight. Drain the water and put the beans in a jar. Twice a day, put a little water in the jar, shake it gently, and then drain out the water. Seedlings use food stored in the bean to grow leaves and roots. In five days, the shoots should be ready to eat in a salad.

► Try growing apple, orange, or watermelon seeds. Soak the seeds in water overnight. Leave the bowl in a warm place. The next day, plant the seeds in twos or threes in small plastic cups full of potting soil. Water them well and put the cups in a warm, dark place until shoots appear. Be patient—fruit tree seeds may take a few weeks to germinate. Keep the soil moist, but don't make it too wet or the seeds may rot. When the plants get larger, you can put them in bigger pots and move them to a sunny place.

LIVING UNDERGROUND

Tubers and **bulbs** are underground food supplies that help some plants survive the winter. The part of the potato we eat is the tuber—the thick part of a plant's underground root. During the winter, the part of the plant above the soil dies. When the weather becomes warm, the potato plant sprouts into new life.

A bulb stores food for a plant in layers of fleshy leaves. Like tubers, bulbs stay alive underground during the winter. When spring arrives, the bulb sends out a shoot, which produces a stem, leaves, and flowers above the ground. Roots grow from the bottom of a bulb.

Place a hyacinth bulb in the neck of a tall jar filled with water so that the bottom of the bulb stays wet. You may need to stick toothpicks in the sides of the bulb to keep the top two-thirds of it out of the water. Leave the jar in a dark place until the shoot is about an inch (25 millimeters) high. Then bring it into direct sunlight. A fragrant flower will grow from the bulb.

A patch of wild bluebells and a field of tulips both grow from bulbs. Gardeners plant tulip bulbs in the fall so they will bloom in the spring.

Many of the vegetables we eat, such as carrots and radishes, are roots that store food for a plant. We also eat some bulbs, including garlic and onions.

LIFE CYCLE

Most plants have roots that absorb minerals and water from the soil. The minerals and water travel from the roots to all parts of the plant through tubes, like blood travels in your body's veins.

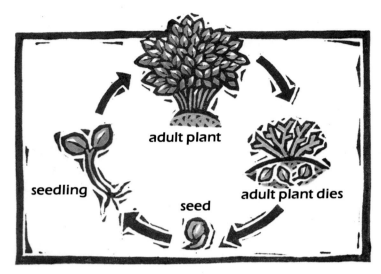

▲ This mountain **conifer** manages to hold on to the thin soil between rock slabs. Roots anchor the tree in the soil and keep it upright.

▲ Over time, a plant uses up lots of minerals from the soil. After the plant dies, it rots and releases these minerals back into the soil. Rotted plant matter is called **compost**. A seed may someday germinate near the spot where the first plant died. The new plant's roots will feed on the minerals left behind.

◄ Dead leaves that fall to the ground also put minerals back into the soil. The leaves rot over several years and make a layer of compost called **leaf mold**. Worms drag some of the leaf mold down into the soil, making the soil richer for new plant roots.

▼ Make some compost to improve the soil in your garden or for your houseplants. Save soft plant matter, such as old potato peelings, and mix it with grass and leaves in a plastic box. Keep the box outdoors. In about five weeks, the mixture will rot into a rich brown compost. Combine it with soil and put your plants in it.

Ask a grown-up to help you peel vegetables so you don't cut yourself.

▲ Chickens scratch on a compost heap looking for food. Farmers use compost to help their crops grow.

TERRIFIC TREES

A tree's sturdy trunk grows above the ground. Trees have protective **bark** that keeps out pests and prevents water loss.

▲ Each spring a tree grows a thick ring of new wood under its bark. A ring of darker wood grows during the summer. Can you tell how old this tree is?

▲ Have you ever sat under a tree on a hot day? Large, leafy trees provide shade for people, animals, houses, and streets.

◀ Make a collection of leaf rubbings. First collect a variety of leaves. Then lay each leaf under a sheet of paper and rub gently with a crayon. Label your rubbings with the name of the tree the leaf came from, and put them in a scrapbook. The library will have books to help you identify trees by their different leaves.

◀ Bark rubbings are easy to make, too. Tape a piece of paper to a tree trunk and rub over it with a crayon.

▼ These flies were trapped in sticky **resin** oozing from tree bark about 30 million years ago. Resin that contains **fossils**, or plant or animal remains, is called amber.

GLORIOUS FOOD

Plants are the main source of food for people around the world. People eat many different parts of plants, including roots, tubers, leaves, seeds, and fruits.

▲ Plants make their own food, but animals must eat other things to stay alive and healthy. **Herbivores** get their food by eating only plants, and **carnivores** are meat eaters. **Omnivores** eat both plants and animals. Most people are omnivores. A cow and a rabbit feed on plants. The animals are eaten by people, who also eat fruits and vegetables.

◀ Seeds provide energy for people and animals. Make a winter pudding for the birds around your home. Mix birdseed in a bowl with suet. Fill an old bowl with the pudding and put it outside on a windowsill or in a bird feeder.

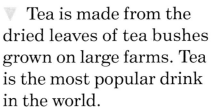

▼ Tea is made from the dried leaves of tea bushes grown on large farms. Tea is the most popular drink in the world.

▲ This woman is planting rice seedlings. Rice is the main food for half of the world's people. Peanuts, peas, beans, and oats are some of the other seeds that we eat.

◄ Fruits and vegetables contain **vitamins**, which help keep us healthy. We often think of tomatoes as vegetables, but if you look at the inside of a tomato, you will discover that it is really a fruit. The red tomato fruit holds and protects the seeds from which new plants will grow. How many fruits and vegetables can you name? Which are your favorites?

COLORS AND FLAVORS

Plants give us many things besides food. We use wood from trees to make homes, paper, and furniture. Rubber comes from the juice of the rubber tree.

► Dyes made from plants have been used for centuries to color cloth and wool. This street shop in Bolivia offers a variety of bright bundles of wool. Some dyes we now use are made with chemicals in a laboratory, but many colors have traditionally come from plant juices.

▼ Herbs and spices make food tasty. They come from different parts of plants, such as seeds, roots, or leaves. This spice, called saffron, comes from crocus flowers.

▲ Ask an adult to boil water and add onion skins, beets, turmeric, or spinach leaves. Boil an egg for five minutes in the water. You can decorate the egg even more by painting it when it is dry.

You can make stationery and gift wrap by dyeing sheets of light-colored paper or thin cardboard. Ask an adult to boil onion skins or beets in a pan. Carefully strain the water into a large, clean bowl. When the water is cool, dip the sheets of paper in it. Hang the dyed paper on a line to dry. Experiment with other brightly colored plants like spinach or rhubarb. What colors do they make? Try leaving the paper in the dye for different amounts of time. Which plant dye do you think works best?

HOTHOUSE

Almost all tropical rain forests grow near the **equator**—the imaginary line around the middle of the Earth. The rain-forest climate is warm and wet. Countless plants and animals live there. The ground, or floor, of a rain forest receives very little sunlight. Most trees must grow very tall to reach the light.

The world's rain forests play a very important role in keeping the Earth's air, water, and weather in proper balance. Trees and other plants clean the air by absorbing carbon dioxide and giving off oxygen.

▲ Smoke and gases pour into the Earth's air from factories, homes, and cars. Each day thousands of acres of rain forests are cut down for wood, farming, or mining. As the rain forests are cut down, extra amounts of carbon dioxide build up in the air. The balance of gases in the air is changing.

◄ Rain forests also act like huge sponges. The plants and trees soak up rainwater with their roots and give off moisture through the holes in their leaves. The air in rain forests is moist and steamy all year long.

► Make a rain-forest bottle-garden and watch the process in action in your own home!

To make your own rain forest, you will need the following:

A spoon with a stick tied to the handle

A large wide-necked jar

Two or three small, slow-growing houseplants, such as:

a polka dot plant

a bead plant

a silver net plant

A tight-fitting lid or cork

Some small pebbles or gravel, rinsed clean

Damp compost

Clean and dry the jar. Cover the bottom with gravel for drainage.

Spoon a thick layer of compost over the gravel. Dig holes in the compost and put the plants in place with the spoon. Pat the compost down around the roots and water the plants.

Seal the jar with the lid or cork and put it in a sunny place. Water the garden only once a month. Mist will form on the glass as water is given off by the plants.

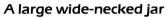

29

GLOSSARY

absorb: to soak up liquid or gas

bark: the protective outer covering of the trunk and branches of a tree

bulb: the thick base of a plant's stem, in which food is stored underground during the winter

carnivore: an animal that eats other animals

chlorophyll: the green substance that plants use to make food from water, carbon dioxide, and energy from sunlight

compost: rotted plant matter that makes soil rich in minerals

conifer: a tree that bears cones, which are filled with seeds

deciduous trees: trees that lose their leaves in the fall

equator: the imaginary line around the middle of the Earth, at an equal distance from the North and South poles

evergreens: trees that have green leaves all year round

fossils: the hardened remains of plants or animals that lived many years ago

fruit: the part of a plant that holds and protects the seed or seeds

germinate: to sprout and begin growing

habitat: the natural home of a living thing or group of living things. A river, a desert, and a rain forest are all habitats.

herbivore: an animal that eats only plant matter

leaf mold: a layer of compost made up of rotted leaves

minerals: non-living substances such as iron and salt. Living things need small amounts of minerals to help them live and grow.

nectar: a sugary liquid produced mainly by flowers and eaten by insects, birds, and bats

omnivore: an animal that eats both plant and animal matter. Most people are omnivores.

photosynthesis: the process of food-making in a plant, involving chlorophyll, sunlight, carbon dioxide, and water

pollen: the powdery substance produced in a flower's stamens. Pollen contains the male cells needed to fertilize the female cells in a flower.

reproduce: to make new plants or animals of the same species

resin: the sticky substance that oozes out and protects the bark of some trees

seed coat: the layer surrounding a seed that protects it

seedling: a young plant grown from a seed

species: a group of plants or animals that are very much like one another

spores: tiny capsules found in some plants that will grow into new plants when released. Mosses and ferns develop from spores.

stamens: the male reproductive parts of a flower. Pollen is produced in stamens.

tuber: a short, thick underground stem that contains a store of food

variegated: marked with different colors

vitamins: substances found in foods, especially fruits and vegetables, that help keep us healthy

INDEX